DAD - THIS JOKE'S FOR YOU

DAD— THIS JOKE'S FOR YOU

THE BEST DAD JOKES
FROM THE FUNNIEST COMEDIANS

edited by **JUDY BROWN**

RONNIE SELLERS gift books PORTLAND, MAINE

Acknowledgements

*First of all, I'd like to thank all those professionally
funny people — the comedians — who have shared their
wit and wisdom about parenting.
And then, of course, I must thank the people
who raise the children of this world.*

Judy Brown

Published by Ronnie Sellers Productions, Inc.

Series Editor: Robin Haywood
Production Editor: Mary Baldwin
Designer: George Corsillo, Design Monsters

P.O. Box 818, Portland, Maine 04104
For ordering information:
Phone: 1-800-MAKE-FUN (800-625-3386)
Fax: (207) 772-6814
Visit our Web site: www.makefun.com
E-mail: rsp@rsvp.com

ISBN: 1-56906-584-5
Library of Congress Control Number: 2004094753

Introduction

Ah, fatherhood. It's eternal — and inescapable.
We all have a father. Many of us are fathers, or will be one.

Scientists have discovered that by the time
a child reaches nursery school age, he or she
will laugh about 300 to 400 times a day,
while adults laugh only an average of 10 to 15 times.

The point of this book, Dad, is to help
you even up those odds.

Have fun,

Judy Brown
judybrowni@usa.net

Section ①

A dad is born

I'm preparing for the baby. I'm busy putting child-proof caps on all the bottles of booze.

—DAVID LETTERMAN

I never loved anyone so much at first meeting. But let's make no mistake why these babies come here: To replace us. We'll see who's wearing the diapers when all this is over.

—JERRY SEINFELD

The sonogram. We had fun looking for early traces of family resemblance. "Gee, honey, it looks just like your mother, if she were bald, had no eyelids, and was floating in amniotic fluid." "Yeah, but from this side, it looks like your father. Presuming, of course, he was a Hawaiian prawn."

—PAUL REISER

Some men actually enjoy changing diapers and doing late-night feedings. We must get to these men and talk sense into them before they ruin everything.

—ALAN THICKE

You take Lamaze classes. I went. It was a total waste of time. Ain't nobody going to breathe a baby out. There's going to be a fight.

—SINBAD

The old system of having a baby was much better than the new system, the old system being characterized by the fact that the man didn't have to watch.

—DAVE BARRY

She's screaming like crazy. You have this myth that you're sharing the birth experience. Unless you're circumcising yourself with a chain saw, I don't think so. Unless you're opening an umbrella up your butt, I don't think so!

—ROBIN WILLIAMS

My wife just let me know I'm about to become a father for the first time. Thank you. The bad news is that we already have two kids.

—BRIAN KILEY

All of that time during the pregnancy when I was supposed to be reading baby books, and taking baby classes, and learning baby CPR didn't go totally to waste because I did use the time to shop for the perfect video camera.

—PAUL REISER

I used my Lamaze breathing when the anesthesiologist's bill came, but it sure didn't work when the real deal was going on. I was breathing in my wife's face when she grabbed me by the throat and shouted in my ear, "If you don't quit breathing that funky breath in my face, and get me some drugs quick, I am going to yank your head off and roll it down the hall!"

—SINBAD

My wife, God bless her, was in labor for 32 hours. And I was faithful to her the entire time.

—JONATHAN KATZ

My baby, "Hesitation Klein," took 20 hours of labor to come out. They used a plunger at the end.

—ROBERT KLEIN

We had a C-section. That's when the baby comes out like toast. It was a blessed event, a wonderful, miraculous thing. But it also showed me what a self-centered dick I am. The doctor says, "We're going to have to perform a C-section. Instead of going, "Oh my God, I hope everything's okay," I thought, "Oh great, I went to Lamaze for nothing." The doctor took my baby out of my wife's stomach. Then he turned to me and asked, "Mr. Goldthwait, would you like to cut the cord?" And I said, "Isn't there anyone more qualified?"

—BOB GOLDTHWAIT

My wife didn't want her drugs until after our daughter was born. I told her, "This is not the Olympics or a gladiator movie. If it starts hurting, take the damn Demerol." **—TIM ALLEN**

My wife showed courage throughout the ordeal of giving birth. Until the end, when she whispered through her clenched teeth, "I want you to come close to me now, honey — so I can grab your testicles and you can understand the pain I'm going through."

—DON WARE

Lamaze expects the husband, me, to be there, so that I can witness this festivity. I did not want to be there. This was remarkably painful for my wife. There was nothing my presence could really do to relieve her pain. In other words, I didn't see why my evening should be ruined too.

—DENNIS WOLFBERG

My son was circumcised by his father. Who's not a doctor, just cheap.

—DARYL HOGUE

Naming our kid was a real trial. I seize up when I have to name a document on my computer.

—JEFF STILSON

In some cultures they don't name their babies right away. They wait until they see how the child develops. Like in *Dances with Wolves*. Unfortunately, our kids' names would be less romantic and poetic. "This is my oldest boy, *'Falls Off His Tricycle,'* his friend, *'Dribbles His Juice,'* and my beautiful daughter, *'Allergic to Nuts.'*"

—PAUL REISER

We gave our children old-fashioned names.
Our little boy is Hunter, and our little girl
is Gatherer.

—BRIAN KILEY

The hardest thing in the world is making a kid
happy after he's been circumcised.

—DAMON WAYANS

Section ②

Bringing home the baby

Having children gives your life purpose.

Right now my purpose is to get some sleep.

—RENO GOODALE

We have a baby now at my house, all day long. And all night long. I wonder why they say you have a baby? The baby has you.

—GALLAGHER

When you're a parent, you're a prisoner of war. You can't go anywhere without paying someone to come and look after your kids. In the old days, baby-sitters charged 50 cents an hour; they'd steam clean the carpet and detail your car. Now they've got their own union. I couldn't afford it, so I had my mother come over. The sitters called her a scab and beat her up on the front lawn.

—ROBERT G. LEE

When my son was born, I had this dream that one day he might grow up to be a Nobel Prize winner. But I also had another dream that he might grow up to say, "Do you want fries with that?"

—ROBIN WILLIAMS

When you're a parent you give up your freedom. You sleep according to someone else's schedule, you eat according to someone else's schedule. It's like being in jail, but you really love the warden.

—LEW SCHNEIDER

Daddy is the guy who's quick to appear with the camera and just as quick to disappear when there's a diaper to be changed.

—JOAN RIVERS

I think God made babies cute so we don't eat them.

—ROBIN WILLIAMS

I'm four hundred and eighty-two months old; can you tell I'm a new father?

—RENO GOODALE

Parents are not interested in justice, they are interested in quiet.

—BILL COSBY

Moms are better at baby talk than dads. Duh. For a dad, baby talk is, "Here, you take him."

—JAY LENO

Husbands are afraid to touch the child at first. The mother learns immediately that you can sling it over your shoulder and it will be just fine. Edgar never changed a diaper; he was very proud of that. As he threw my child through the air he'd say, "She's wet."

—JOAN RIVERS

When I was a baby, I cried an awful lot, but my mother said she wouldn't change me for a million. My father said, "Maybe if you'd change him, he'd stop crying."

—HENNY YOUNGMAN

It's important for husbands to know when to change a diaper. I figure every three days is about right.

—ALAN THICKE

I became a father. There's a lot to do with kids. I had to hold him, pat him on the back, and burp him. Luckily I've had a lot of practice on my mom.

—DAVID LETTERMAN

Shouldn't there be some kind of relationship between how much a baby eats and how much comes out the other end? It's like at the circus, where they've got the tiny VW bug but the clowns just keep coming out and out and out . . . Eventually you learn how to hold your breath like a Hokkaido pearl diver.

—DENNIS MILLER

You have got to change those diapers every day. When it says six to twelve pounds on the side of the Pampers box, they're not lying. That's all those things will hold.

—JEFF FOXWORTHY

Baby ca-ca is like Kryptonite to a father. Even the dog says "You don't rub *his* face in it."

—ROBIN WILLIAMS

From the jump, I was a high-tech daddy. I had this cool mountain backpack to carry my kids in. I was able to take them with me everywhere. The only drawback to the backpack is that babies pour acidic Similac down your neck. But at least I have no more back hair.

—SINBAD

My friend has a sixteen-month-old. The baby's crawling around and he has an accident in his diaper. And the mother comes over and says, "Isn't that adorable? Brandon made a gift for Daddy." I'm thinking this guy must be real easy to shop for on Father's Day.

—GARRY SHANDLING

What's the best way to keep two-year-old children from biting their fingernails? Make them change their own diapers.

—PAUL LYNDE

The best device we have in our house is the baby intercom, a kind of walkie-talkie that lets you monitor your kid from other rooms. So my daughter's in the crib with one part of the intercom, and I'm in the other. Then all of a sudden, I hear her crackling over the static, "Breaker, one-nine, Daddy. I've got spit-up on my shirt and I'm packing a load. Please, come help me out."

—BOB SAGET

Section ③

The joys of fatherhood

A two-year-old is like having a blender,
but you don't have a top for it.

—JERRY SEINFELD

If the new American father feels bewildered and even defeated, let him take comfort from the fact that whatever he does in any fathering situation has a 50 percent chance of being right.

—BILL COSBY

I have two-year-old twins in my house, it's nuts. I make excuses to get out, "Honey, you need anything from anywhere? Anything from the Motor Vehicle bureau? C'mon, let me register something. I was going out anyway, to apply for jury duty. Please!"

—RAY ROMANO

The baby is great. My wife and I have just started potty training. Which I think is important, because when we wanna potty-train the baby we should set an example.

—HOWIE MANDEL

When I was a baby, my father used to throw me up in the air and then answer the phone.

—RITA RUDNER

I called a friend and his three-year-old answered the phone. "My Daddy is the best daddy in the world. My Daddy took me to the animal zoo. I love my Daddy." He got on the phone. I said, "Carl, enjoy her while she's stupid."

—BOB ALPER

I was raised by my father since birth. He's been both mother and father to me. I call him Smother. He still lactates whenever he hears a baby cry.

—KAITLIN COLOMBO

You have a baby, you have to clean up your act. You can't come in drunk and go, "Hey, here's a little switch, Daddy's going to throw up on you."

—ROBIN WILLIAMS

My child jammed 75 raisins up her nose. I mean jammed so tight she couldn't breathe, but she wouldn't let on, afraid I'd be mad. Just sitting on a raisin box trying to act cool.

—SINBAD

I love being a dad. But the job is not without certain details that make me want to remove my clothes, climb City Hall, and make bird calls until I'm hauled off to some nice, safe place where I can't hurt myself.

—MICHAEL BURKETT

Raising a child may be a labor of love, but nonetheless, it is a job. Usually a fun job. But sometimes so frustrating, menial, and dull, it makes working the corn dog concession in the Ringworm Brothers Carnival seem like a stint in the double-O sector of Her Majesty's Secret Service.

—DENNIS MILLER

If the children's name for me is "Dad-Can-I" then my name for them is "Yes-You-May."

—BILL COSBY

A mother will go to the store for bread and milk and return with enough groceries to feed Bangladesh for a year. A father will go to the store for bread and milk and return with bread, nacho-flavored Doritos, and five dollars' worth of lottery tickets.

—MICHAEL BURKETT

I'd been giving my kids Flintstones vitamins, but then I realized that Fred and Barney weren't exactly the pictures of health.

—BUZZ NUTLEY

The worst thing that can happen to a man is to have his wife come home and find out that he has lost the child. "How did everything go?" "Great, we're playing hide and seek, and she's winning."

—SINBAD

Mothers wash dishes after every meal. Fathers wash dishes when the sink is so full that you have to go to the bathroom for a glass of water.

—MICHAEL BURKETT

Fathers are the geniuses of the house because only a person as intelligent as we could fake such stupidity. Think about your father: he doesn't know where anything is, you ask him to do something, he messes it up, so your mother sends you, "Go down and see what your father's doing before he blows up the house." He's a genius at work because he doesn't want to do it, and knows someone will be coming soon to stop him.

—BILL COSBY

All the other parents who have children my daughter's age are ten to twenty years younger than I am, and are tattooed and pierced. When I meet them for a play date with our kids, I feel like I should be baby-sitting them, too. "Where do you think you're going with hair that color, young man?"

—RENO GOODALE

Sex after children slows down. Every three months now we have sex. Every time I have sex, the next day I pay my quarterly taxes. Unless it's oral sex, then I renew my driver's license.

—RAY ROMANO

These kids are nuts today. I got a kid myself, ten years old. He's going to be eleven, if I let him!

—HENNY YOUNGMAN

In a nutshell, just be good and kind to your children because not only are they the future of the world, they are the ones who can eventually sign you into the home.

—DENNIS MILLER

People have always told me that I'd learn more from my kids than they'd learn from me. I believe that. I've learned that as a parent, when you have sex your body emits a hormone that drifts down the hall into your child's room and makes them want a drink of water.

—JEFF FOXWORTHY

My father looked at kids as additions to his tool kit. He got me, apparently, after thinking, "Oh, it's snowing again. I'll go back to bed and make a little snow-shoveling machine."

—BOB ODENKIRK

Is your teenage son or daughter out for the evening? If so, take advantage of the opportunity. Pack your furniture, call a moving van, and don't leave a forwarding address.

—KENNY YOUNGMAN

My mother said the best time to ask my dad for anything was when he was having sex. Not the best advice I've ever been given.

—JIMMY CARR

I spent a week at a Buddhist monastic retreat, where I sat silently for hours at a time in an uncomfortable position trying to shatter my ego. Why bother? Two minutes with my wife and kids does the same thing.

—BRIAN KOFFMAN

We don't hit our kids, we use the time out, because it works so well in professional hockey. My son is 13 and as tall as I am, so I'm real happy that I don't hit him. As it is, I'm afraid that when I'm 60 he's going to hold me down and tickle me until I pee.

—JACK COEN

Don't ever raise your hands to your kids. It leaves your groin unprotected.

—RED BUTTONS

I've got good kids, I love my kids. I'm trying to bring them up the right way, not spanking them. I find waving the gun around gets the same job done.

—DENIS LEARY

Since childhood is a time when kids prepare to be grown-ups, I think it makes a lot of sense to completely traumatize your children. Gets 'em ready for the real world.

—GEORGE CARLIN

Children are smarter than any of us. Know how I know that? I don't know one child with a full-time job and children.

—BILL HICKS

The thing I have the most trouble with is trying to discipline my little guy, because everything he does makes me laugh, and you don't want to send the wrong message. Like last week he'd somehow gotten hold of a carving knife and he was stabbing my in-laws repeatedly. It was funny, but I had to be like, "No, that's bad."

—BRIAN KILEY

My father used to ground me, and then run electricity through me.

—TAYLOR NEGRON

The face of a child can say it all, especially the mouth part of the face.

—JACK HANDY

I like my kids a lot, but it's like a rodeo clown car pulled up and 15 of them got out and they're running around. It's like they're monkeys on acid and they're hanging on lamps and lights and the ceiling. Get down!

—DENIS LEARY

In schools, you can always identify the children who were dressed by their fathers. Such children should have signs pinned to their strange attire that say, "Please do not scorn or mock me. I was dressed by my father, who sees colors the way Beethoven heard notes."

—BILL COSBY

It's a myth that you will be able to help your children with their homework. I'm taking remedial math so I can help my son make it to the third grade.

—SINBAD

My kid drives me nuts. For three years now he goes to a private school, he won't tell me where it is.

—RODNEY DANGERFIELD

Let's face it, by the second grade you can no longer do the math. We didn't have that stuff in college. It is truly a shame when your seven-year-old son says, "Daddy, will you check my math?" and you have to lie and say, "I trust you, son."

—SINBAD

Having children is like having a bowling alley in your brain.

—MARTIN MULL

My father is a doctor, with the worst hand-writing. He wrote me a note once excusing me from gym class. I gave it to my teacher, and she gave me all of her money.

—RITA RUDNER

My kid is a born doctor. He can't write any-thing anybody can read.

—HENNY YOUNGMAN

Section ④

Whatever you say, dad

A tornado touched down, uprooting a large tree in the front yard, demolishing the house across the street. Dad went to the door, opened it, surveyed the damage, muttered "Darn kids!" and closed the door.

—TIM CONWAY

"Don't get smart with me," my father would growl. That was my favorite expression of his. Don't get smart with me. Just once I wanted to make a weird face and go, "Duh! Is this dumb enough for you, dad?"

—LOUIE ANDERSON

My son has a new nickname for me, "Baldy." Son, I've got a new word for you, "Heredity."

—DAN SAVAGE

My father was a cop, so dating was a nightmare. I could handle the police escort, but the bullhorn from the helicopter was a bit much: "Son, keep your hands on the steering wheel where we can see them."

—SANDI SELVI

I remember the days when it was fashionable to spank your child. My father would say to me, "This hurts me worse than it does you." I wanted to say, "Then you bend over, and I'll lighten your emotional load, buddy."

—LIZ SELLS

My efforts to say nothing but positive things to my son have become desperate. "You're the best, smartest, cutest, friendliest baby, you're . . . telekinetic. You move objects with thought and start fires with your brain."

—ANDY DICK

I phoned my dad to tell him I had stopped smoking. He called me a quitter.

—STEVEN PEARL

Now that I'm a dad, I'm sure my father is laughing in his grave. I used to ask my father, "Dad, where did all those wrinkles come from on your face?" "From you, your little brother, and your goddamn sister."

—JACK COEN

My dad said I'd never amount to anything. Lucky guess.

—DAVID COUSINS

Once, when I was a kid, another kid made a racial slur and I told my dad about it. I'll never forget what my dad told me: "Greg, it doesn't matter what race you are or the color of your skin. There will always be some people out there who aren't gonna like you because you're irritating."

—GREG ROGELL

My son complains about headaches. I tell him all the time, "When you get out of bed, it's feet first!"

—HENNY YOUNGMAN

I once complained to my father that I didn't seem to be able to do things the same way other people did. Dad's advice? "Margo, don't be a sheep. People hate sheep. They eat sheep."

—MARGO KAUFMAN

My dad is not real bright, but I love the guy. We go into this trophy shop because my basketball team won second place, and there are trophies everywhere. My dad looks around and goes, "This guy is really good."

—FRED WOLF

After watching the Kevorkian trial I asked my father, "Do you think a family should have the right to withdraw life support on a loved one?" He said, "It depends on which kid."

—HUGH FINK

I went to college, majored in Philosophy. My father said, "Why don't you minor in Communications so you can wonder out loud?

—MIKE DUGAN

My kids bring their friends around and say, "We can tell how old our daddy is by counting the rings on his stomach."

—TONY KORNHEISER

With my old man I got no respect. I asked him, "How can I get my kite in the air?" He told me to run off a cliff.

—RODNEY DANGERFIELD

My father took me to the zoo. He told me to go over to the leopard and play connect the dots.

—RODNEY DANGERFIELD

My father used to talk to me. He'd say, "Listen, stupid." He always called me "Listen."

—HENNY YOUNGMAN

I bought my father an answering machine. He still hasn't figured out how to leave an outgoing message. You call my father's house . . . ring, ring, ring, click, "God damn it, Mary, how in the hell do you use this stupid piece of shit? Come over here and look and see if you can help me with the . . . beep!"

—ROSIE O'DONNELL

When I was a kid I asked my dad if I could go ice skating. He told me to wait until it gets warmer.

—RODNEY DANGERFIELD

Section ⑤

Dad on wheels

Wherever we had to be, we were usually late because Dad was always implementing some plan or theory to avoid traffic.

—RAY ROMANO

When you're a dad you can't keep your cool car. Fancy stereo, power windows, sunroof; the kids are going to kill all that stuff. Take an ordinary cookie. In the hands of a kid it becomes a sugar hand grenade. You have to take the car into the shop because chocolate chips are clogging the carburetor.

—SINBAD

Dads never want anyone else to drive. Mine especially. On his way out the door, he'd announce, "I'll do the goddamn driving. I was in a war!"

—LOUIE ANDERSON

I think the dilemma of being a 13-year-old girl is best summed up by a book I've heard about, titled something like *I Hate You and I Wish You Would Die, but First, Can You Drive Me to the Mall?*

—TONY KORNHEISER

My dad didn't like people as much as he liked his car. He even introduced it to people, "It's my Bonneville," he said. "My family's over there."

—LOUIE ANDERSON

When his child requests a car, a father will wish that he were a member of some sect that hasn't gone beyond the horse. "Dad, all my friends say that I should have my own car," the boy says earnestly one day. "Wonderful. When are they going to buy it?"

—BILL COSBY

My father drives so slow. Once a cop stopped my father, "Sir, do you know how fast you were driving? Three miles an hour." "Sorry officer, I guess I was a little anxious." To do what? Simulate time-lapse photography?

—CATHY LADMAN

I live in Los Angeles. It's kind of scary. What do I do as a parent if someday my son wants to join a gang? Do I car pool drive-by shootings?

—ROBERT G. LEE

There exists a widespread folk myth that humans should learn about sex from their parents. My relationship with my father nearly ended when he tried to teach me how to drive. I can't imagine our relationship having survived his instructing me how to operate my penis.

—BOB SMITH

I'm a grown woman but my father still thinks I know nothing about my car. He always asks me, "You changing the oil every 3,000?" "Yes, Dad. I'm also putting sugar in the gas tank. That way my exhaust smells like cotton candy."

—MIMI GONZALEZ

Me and my dad used to play tag. He'd drive!

—RODNEY DANGERFIELD

My father's not a warm and fuzzy guy. He can't bring himself to ask about my feelings or emotions. All he ever asks is, "How's the car doing?" Finally, I said, "The car is experiencing low self-esteem and financial distress. The car could use a new computer, and probably, a new car."

—DANA EAGLE

Section ⑥

Mr. big spender

You know what a Dad is?
An ATM with pants.

—JOHN DAVID SIDLEY

My childhood was rough. Once for my birthday, my old man gave me a bat. The first day I played with it, it flew away.

—RODNEY DANGERFIELD

I put my tooth under my pillow with dreams of a quarter in my head. I woke up in the middle of the night, and there was my father with his hand under the pillow. I believed in the tooth fairy, so I thought she had been there already and my father was ripping me off, and I bit him. The next night I had two more teeth to put under my pillow.

—A. WHITNEY BROWN

My husband is so cheap, on Christmas Eve
he fires one shot and tells the kids Santa
committed suicide.

—PHYLLIS DILLER

My father was so cheap that one year he told
us Santa didn't come because he wears red
and we lived in a Crips zone.

—A.J. JAMAL

They say when you die there's a light at the end of the tunnel. When my father dies, he'll see the light, make his way toward it, and then flip it off to save electricity.

—HARLAND WILLIAMS

My father was so cheap. For Easter, we'd wear the same clothes, but he'd take us to a different church.

—A.J. JAMAL

It was tough asking thrifty parents for money. You've got to beg fathers: "Dad, can I have a dollar?" "What happened to the dollar I gave you last year?"

—SINBAD

I've spent a fortune on my kids' education, and a fortune on their teeth. The difference is, they use their teeth.

—ROBERT ORBEN

When I was about ten we moved, because my father sold our house. Somehow the landlord found out about it and we had to go.

—A. WHITNEY BROWN

My family was homeless for a long time. I grew up in Canada, so I thought we had just gone camping. And my parents kept me in the dark, because they were embarrassed. I'd ask, "Dad, are we living below the poverty line?" And he'd say, "No son, we're rich as long as we have each other. Now get in the dumpster."

—JIM CARREY

My father refused to spend money on me as a kid. One time I broke my arm playing football and my father tried to get a free X-ray by taking me down to the airport and making me lie down with the luggage.

—GLENN SUPER

My dad always maintained he didn't care about money. That's because he never had any.

—LOUIE ANDERSON

My father was cheap. Every year he'd say "I'm glad Christmas comes but once every other year."

—JOHN ROY

My father was so cheap. We'd eat Hamburger Helper with no hamburger.

—A.J. JAMAL

My dad's so cheap. He's always yelling at me for spending money. "Look at you, spending money, you're such a big shot." Oh, yeah, buying food, paying rent. I'm just showing off.

—CATHY LADMAN

My father was so cheap that when I was a teenager and I wanted to speak to my friends on the phone, my father was hovering over me shouting, "Keep it brief! Keep it brief!" Our phone bills were so miniscule, I swear that if Alexander Graham Bell had seen one of them he would have said, "There's no money in this."

—CATHY LADMAN

My father makes money the American way. He trips over stuff and sues people.

—DOMINIC DIERKES

Section 7

Dad– this joke's for you

Fatherhood is pretending the present you love most is soap-on-a-rope.

—BILL COSBY

My father's a strange guy. He's allergic to cotton. He has pills he's supposed to take, but he can't get them out of the bottle.

—BRIAN KILEY

My dad is waiting to buy new clothes until he loses weight. So he's still wearing his Cub Scout uniform.

—RITA RUDNER

I grew up in a big family, six kids. Seven, if you count my dad. Man, he got all the attention, being the youngest.

—MARGARET SMITH

I want a guy just like my dad, who orders dentures through the mail, and takes great pride in the fact that his eyebrows meet.

—JUDY TENUTA

My mom has been nagging my father to take up a sport, so he took up birdwatching. He's very serious about it. He bought binoculars. And a bird.

—RITA RUDNER

Whenever I come home from playing golf, my son always asks me excitedly, "Did you win, Dad?" I have explained to him time and time again that you're really just playing against yourself. This time the family was on vacation and I had gone out to play a round. When I returned, the kids were swimming in the hotel pool, which was full of young kids and surrounded by dozens of parents. From across the pool, at the top of his lungs, my son yelled, "Hey, Dad! Were you just playing with yourself?" We checked out that night.

—RAY ROMANO

My father is so impatient. He stands in front of the microwave going, "C'mon! It's been ten seconds! I don't have all minute!"

—CATHY LADMAN

Got to be a hell of a man to raise another man's seed. Joseph was Jesus' stepdaddy. How the hell do you tell Jesus what to do? "I don't feel like cleaning my room. And you don't want me calling my real daddy." "O.K., we'll clean your room, Jesus. We don't want it raining 40 days and 40 nights in here."

—D.L. HUGHLEY

There are no perfect parents. Even Jesus had a distant father and a domineering mother. I'd have trust issues if my father allowed me to be crucified.

—BOB SMITH

When my son graduated from college he went directly into what I like to call the international food-service industry. Delivering for a pizzeria.

—BOB ALPER

I never know what to get my father for his birthday. I gave him $100 and said, "Buy yourself something that will make your life easier." So he bought a present for my mother.

—RITA RUDNER

My father wanted me to become a doctor, but I wanted to do something that required more imagination. So we compromised and I became a hypochondriac.

—WALLY WANG

Something happens when a man reaches a certain age, "The News" becomes the most important thing in his life. All fathers think one day they're going to get a call from the State Department. "Listen, we've completely lost track of the situation in the Middle East. You've been watching the news. What do you think we should do about it?"

—JERRY SEINFELD

My Dad went back to college and we're all so proud of him. Except when he comes home from a keg party and pees out the window.

—BRIAN KILEY

My parents live in the Central Time Zone. I talk to my father once a week, but he still doesn't understand time zones, "Well it's eight o'clock here, so what is it, six o'clock there, huh, huh? It's summer here, so what is it, winter there? It's the Industrial Revolution here, so is it the Paleolithic era there?"

—HUGH FINK

Do you know what someone said to me last week? They told me I looked like my dad. Just what every girl wants to hear, "You look a lot like a middle-aged, overweight Italian man, with a moustache."

—LORI GIANELLA

According to my dad he had a really tough child-hood. He had to walk 20 miles to school in five feet of snow, and he was only four feet tall.

—DANA EAGLE

Dad was a kidder. Whenever I misbehaved, he'd bury me in the backyard. Only up to my waist, but you get dizzy with all the blood rushing to your head.

—EMO PHILIPS

My father was very hairy. When my brother and I were little, he'd like to amuse us by lighting his chest hairs on fire and then blow them out. Still not conclusive proof that I come from carnie people.

—GRACE WHITE

All fathers are intimidating, because they're fathers. Once a man has children, his attitude is, "To hell with the world, I can make my own people. I'll eat whenever I want, I'll wear whatever I want, and I'll create whoever I want."

—JERRY SEINFELD

When you're young, you think your dad is Superman. Then you grow up, and you realize he's just a regular guy who wears a cape.

—DAVE ATTELL

I'm the father of teenage girls, which means I have only one job: to embarrass my daughters. But I do it with pride. When the guy comes over for a date, I say "Hey, come on in, I'll show you a video of the first time she went potty. I've got it cued up on the VCR."

—JOHN DAVID SIDLEY

My father wore the pants in the family.
At least, after the court order.

—VERNON CHAPMAN

If you ever want to torture my dad, tie him up and right in front of him, refold a road map incorrectly.

—CATHY LADMAN